BOOKS BY J. D. McCLATCHY

Poetry
TEN COMMANDMENTS *1998*
THE REST OF THE WAY *1990*
STARS PRINCIPAL *1986*
SCENES FROM ANOTHER LIFE *1981*

Essays
TWENTY QUESTIONS *1998*
WHITE PAPER *1989*

As Editor
THE VINTAGE BOOK OF CONTEMPORARY
    WORLD POETRY *1996*
WOMAN IN WHITE: POEMS BY EMILY
    DICKINSON *1991*
THE VINTAGE BOOK OF CONTEMPORARY
    AMERICAN POETRY *1990*
POETS ON PAINTERS *1988*
RECITATIVE: PROSE BY JAMES MERRILL *1986*
ANNE SEXTON: THE POET AND HER CRITICS *1978*

1. _____

2. _____

3. _____

4. _____

5. _____

6. _____

7. _____

8. _____

9. _____

10. _____

POEMS BY

J . D . McCLATCHY

ALFRED A. KNOPF   NEW YORK   1998

1. _____

2. _____

3. _____

4. _____

5. _____

6. _____

7. _____

8. _____

9. _____

10. C O M M A N D M E N T S

THIS IS A BORZOI BOOK
PUBLISHED BY ALFRED A. KNOPF, INC.

www.randomhouse.com

Some of these poems originally appeared as follows:
Green Mountains Review: "Bodies"
New England Review: "Variations on Lines Cancelled by Dickinson"
The New Republic: "Honest Iago"
The New Yorker: "My Early Hearts," "Found Parable," "Late Night Ode"
The Paris Review: "Proust in Bed," *"Whatever dreams of escape may cast their spell,"* "Chott"
Poetry: "Dervish," "Lines on My Face," "My Mammogram," "Under Hydra," "Flies," "The Dialogue of Desire and Guilt," "Three Dreams About Elizabeth Bishop"
Poetry Ireland Review: "Sniper"
Press: "Pantoum," "What They Left Behind"
Princeton University Library Chronicle: "Bonhoeffer writes: 'Temptation leads us not' "
Raritan: "Auden's O E D "
The Southwest Review: "Descartes' Dream"
Speak: "Stolen Hours"
"After Ovid" first appeared in *After Ovid: New Metamorphoses,* ed. Michael Hoffmann and James Lasdun (Farrar, Straus and Giroux, 1994).
"After Magritte" first appeared in *Lines/Lignes, Réflexions/Reflections* (The Armand Hammer Museum of Art and Cultural Center, 1997).
"Auden's O E D " was delivered as the 1995 Phi Beta Kappa poem at Connecticut College.

Library of Congress Cataloging-in-Publication Data
McClatchy, J.D., 1945–
Ten Commandments : poems / by J.D. McClatchy.
p.   cm.
ISBN 0-375-40137-7
I. Title.
PS3563.A26123T46   1998
811'.54—dc21   97-49451   CIP

Manufactured in the United States of America
First Edition

FOR CHIP KIDD

CONTENTS

1. _____

2. _____

3. _____

4. _____

5. _____

6. _____

7. _____

8. _____

9. _____

10. _____

1. THOU SHALT HAVE NONE OTHER GODS BUT ME

_____

2. _____

3. _____

4. _____

5. _____

6. _____

7. _____

8. _____

9. _____

10. _____

"God spoke one and I heard two."
That is, he heard himself as well.
Can what I say be also true?
Shaky grounds on which to dwell.
I'd say that angels still rebel
Against authority. And you?

DERVISH

Everything revolves:

          the dreams of the body,

the blood, the earth itself,

          a man's coming from it

and his return.

          In their tombstone caps

and flaring shroud skirts,

          the dervishes spin

toward that moment

          when monotony and ecstasy,

knowing and unknowing

          are the same, planets

wheeled around some

          spindle disguised

as the five-petalled rose

          on a tile underfoot

in a weightless self-regard

          meant to worship the power

that keeps them in motion.

          From a corbelled balcony

the choir's melisma

          twists on a lost soul:

oud and heartbeat,

          the drummed air lifting.

This one—so close

          he brushes against

the fanatic's prayer—

          arms open to anything,

right hand pointing up,

          eyes caught by his left hand,

which he's turned downward

        as if toward the rapture

of, at last, submission . . .

        here is our world.

It is time now to come back

        to the work of creation.

High over the planets

        a golden whiplash script

around the inmost rim

        of today's great dome

calls down: God

        is the light of the heavens,

a niche wherein is a lamp.

        The lamp is in glass.

The glass is a high,

        brightening, constant

star.

MY OLD IDOLS

I. AT TEN

1955. A scratchy waltz
Buzzed over the ice rink's P.A.
My classmate Tony, the barber's son: "Alls
He wantsa do is, you know, like, play."

Bored with perfecting my languid figure eights,
I trailed him to a basement door marked GENTS
With its metal silhouette of high-laced skates
(Symbols, I guess, of methods desire invents).

Tony's older brother was waiting inside.
I'd been "requested," it seemed. He was sixteen,
Tall, rawboned, blue-eyed,
Thumbs hooked into faded, tightening jeans.

I fumbled with small talk, pretending to be shy.
Looking past me, he slowly unzipped his fly.

II. CALLAS

Her voice: steeped in a rancid syrupy phlegm:
Whatever's not believed remains a grace
While again she invokes the power that yields:
Splintered timber and quick consuming flame:
The simplest way to take hold of the heart's
Complications, its pool of spilt religion:
A long black hair sweat-stuck to the skin:
The bitter sleep of the dying: the Jew in Berlin:

Who sent you here? the sharp blade pleads:
Stormcloud: thornhedge: starchill:
Blood bubble floating to the top of the glass:
The light, from fleshrise to soulset:
The world dragging the slow weight of its shame
Like the train of pomp: guttering candle: her voice.

III. IN CLASS

Parasangs, satraps, the daily drill . . .
Beginner's Greek its own touchstone.
The sophomore teacher was Father Moan,
Whom I longed to have praise my skill.
The illustrated reader's best
Accounts of murder and sacrifice
Only suggested the heavy price
I longed to pay at his behest.

He'd slap the pointer against his thigh.
I quivered. What coldness may construe
Of devotion was an experience
As hard to learn as catch his eye.
I kept my hand up. *Here!* I knew
The right answer. The case. The tense.

BETRAYAL

My contempt for your weakness
began with the pointless jealousies.

Underneath your bed I answered for you once,
your panic, your longing, your despair,
while he climbed on you and stuffed your mouth.

Week after week I've had to watch
the old needle tracks and the new habits—
aerobics, twelve-step meetings, the soup kitchen—
so where you used to speak in tongues,
now it's day-glo bumper stickers,
meaning given way to motto.

The arrogant, anorexic young pharaoh
spent his few years building a tomb
to carry his glory into a glass case.
And your mild, hunched-over interest
in it all? Oh, complicity's blurred label.

Did your doubts about me finally seduce you?
Carried on in empty hours as strategically
located as safe houses, and as casually seedy,
the low-wattage affairs, first secret, later flaunted,
you thought a sort of cautious equilibrium
only provoked me to shrug off in silence
the humiliation of living with someone
who is, drinks knocked back, "devoted" to me.

Each has his own god to worship,
little candles, little powers,

the old family snapshot on Sinai,
the maverick at the top of the ladder,
the poolside pair of golden calves.
Choose one and betray the others.

At last you suggested we both take lovers
but continue to live "officially" together,
long evenings spent comparing notes
on the young scapegoats sent into our desert.
Did you think we were jockeying for position,
determined to influence the turn of events,
to subsidize feelings and control the world?
Poor fool, in love with an image of yourself!
In the end you even came to believe in yourself,
your sensible advice and reasonable demands,
as the burning bush might have mistaken its flowers
for flames or the rustling in its spindly branches
for the indrawn, unreliable voice of God.

1. _____

**THOU SHALT NOT MAKE TO THYSELF
ANY GRAVEN IMAGE**
2. _____

3. _____

4. _____

5. _____

6. _____

7. _____

8. _____

9. _____

10. _____

Toothless and gibbering about his gift
From an unjust God, satiric Swift
Was in the end calmly conveyed
To the charitable asylum he'd made
His cause as a young, idealistic dean.
Every day there he stood between
A mirror and the windowed sky,
Stared at himself to multiply
His torment and, wiping the greasy tips
Of his shoes or pursing his swollen lips
With the vanity of a courtesan,
Would mutter, "Poor old man!"

MY EARLY HEARTS

The over-crayoned valentine FOЯ MOTHEЯ.
    The furtive gym-class crush.
In my missal the polychrome Sacred Heart
    Our Savior exposes,
The emblems of his Passion still festering,
    The knotted scourge, the sponge,
The nailhead studs all sweating blood from inside
    A little crown of thorns
Tightening around my groin as I pulled back
    The crushed-velvet curtain
And entered the confessional's dark chamber.
    Whatever lump in the throat
Aztec horror tales had once contrived to raise
    Melted in the aftermath
Of eating—myself both high priest and victim
    On his knees, head yanked back—
The live, quivering heart of thwarted romance,
    A taste one swallowed hard
First to acquire, and much later to mock.
    Hearts bid on, hearts broken.
The shape of a flame reversed in the Zippo
    Cupped close to light one last
Cigarette before walking out on a future.
    The shape two fat, rain-soaked
Paperbacks assumed on the back-porch table
    After I'd left for home,
That whole summer spent reading Tolstoy, sleeping
    With my window open
Onto an imaginary grove of birch—
    One of which I had carved
Two names on and sat under with my diary
    To watch the harvesting.

There is a black heart somewhere—the clarinet
    In K. 581,
Still aching for the pond edge, the rippling pain,
    The god's quick grasp of things.
A white one, too—that teardrop pearl on Vermeer's
    Girl at the Frick, hanging
Above her interrupted letter, mirror
    To what she's left unsaid.

At ten, on a grade-school excursion downtown
    To the science museum,
I learned my lesson once and for all—how to
    Lose myself in a heart.
In that case, a cavernous, walk-through model
    With narrow, underlit
Arterial corridors and piped-in thumps.
    As so often later,
The blindfold loosely fastened by loneliness
    Seemed to help me stumble
Past the smeary diagrams and push-button
    Explanations, helped me
Ignore the back-of-the-closet, sour-milk
    Smells and the silly jokes
Of classmates in the two-story lung next door.
    For those others, the point
Was to end up only where they had begun,
    Back at the start of something,
Eager for the next do-it-yourself gadget.
    I stayed behind, inside,
Under the mixed blessing of not being missed.
    I could hear the old nun
Scolding some horseplay, more faintly leading them
    On to a further room,
"Where a giant pendulum will simulate
    The crisscrossed Sands of Time. . . ."

What had time to do with anything *I* wanted!
 At last I had the heart
All to myself, my name echoing through it
 As I called to myself
In a stage whisper from room to blood-red room.
 And what of the smaller,
Racing heart—my own, that is—inside the heart
 Whose very emptiness
Had by now come to seem a sort of shelter?
 Was it—*me*, I mean, *my* heart—
Even back then ready to stake everything,
 To endure the trials
By fire and water, to pledge long silence,
 Accept the surprises
And sad discoveries one loses his way
 Among, walking around
And around his own heart, looking for a way
 That leads both in and out?

It happens first in one's own heart, doesn't it?
 And then in another's.
Something happens when you hear it happening.
 One day, out of the blue,
An old friend shows up and needs, so you'd thought, just
 A shoulder to cry on.
Or a new friend is stirring in the next room.
 Or the stranger in bed
Beside you gets up in the middle of the night.
 You listen for the steps.
Unfamiliar steps are coming closer, close
 Enough to reach out for.
Come over here, love. Bend down and put your head
 To my chest. Now listen.
Listen. Do you hear them? After all this time
 There are your own footsteps.
Can you hear yourself walking toward me now?

LINES ON MY FACE

Decades now of looking back at it—
in some old satellite's rearview mirror, say—
has something to show beyond the folds and feeders,
the volumes of magma risen into native rock
or the buried flow of old fires cooling
in ocean beds. The damage has been memorized.
Tool marks left by loose doubts dragged
across a certainty. Tongues of river
sediment slumped but still flickering
in the eye. And how pale the surfaces are!

From miles above what even to others is familiar,
the erosion—tears that freeze and crack
the heart, small habits a wind blasts
against whatever's exposed—seems apparent:
all's worn down, weathered, notched, seeping,
yet eerily polished, as if at last defined.
Your map of me? Let your pencil trace
the old quarries and splintered outcrops,
let it analyze the faults, describe their throes,
let it reveal how the light is laid over them all.

MY MAMMOGRAM

I.

In the shower, at the shaving mirror or beach,
For years I'd led . . . the unexamined life?
When all along and so easily within reach
(Closer even than the nonexistent wife)

Lay the trouble—naturally enough
Lurking in a useless, overlooked
Mass of fat and old newspaper stuff
About matters I regularly mistook

As a horror story for the opposite sex,
Nothing to do with what at my downtown gym
Are furtively ogled as The Guy's Pecs.

But one side is swollen, the too tender skin
Discolored. So the doctor orders an X-
Ray, and nervously frowns at my nervous grin.

II.

Mammography's on the basement floor.
The nurse has an executioner's gentle eyes.
I start to unbutton my shirt. She shuts the door.
Fifty, male, already embarrassed by the size

Of my "breasts," I'm told to put the left one
Up on a smudged, cold, Plexiglas shelf,
Part of a robot half menacing, half glum,
Like a three-dimensional model of the Freudian self.

(17)

Angles are calculated. The computer beeps.
Saucers close on a flatness further compressed.
There's an ache near the heart neither dull nor sharp.

The room gets lethal. Casually the nurse retreats
Behind her shield. Anxiety as blithely suggests
I joke about a snapshot for my Christmas card.

I I I .

"No sign of cancer," the radiologist swans
In to say—with just a hint in his tone
That he's done me a personal favor—whereupon
His look darkens. "But what these pictures show . . .

Here, look, you'll notice the gland on the left's
Enlarged. See?" I see an aerial shot
Of Iraq, and nod. "We'll need further tests,
Of course, but I'd bet that what *you've* got

Is a liver problem. Trouble with your estrogen
Levels. It's time, my friend, to take stock.
It happens more often than you'd think to men."

Reeling from its millionth scotch on the rocks,
In other words, my liver's sensed the end.
Why does it come as something less than a shock?

I V .

The end of life as I've known it, that is to say—
Testosterone sported like a power tie,
The matching set of drives and dreads that may
Now soon be plumped to whatever new designs

My apparently resentful, androgynous
Inner life has on me. Blind seer?
The Bearded Lady in some provincial circus?
Something that others both desire and fear.

Still, doesn't everyone *long* to be changed,
Transformed to, no matter, a higher or lower state,
To know the leathery D-Day hero's strange

Detachment, the queen bee's dreamy loll?
Yes, but the future each of us blankly awaits
Was long ago written on the genetic wall.

v .

So suppose the breasts fill out until I look
Like my own mother . . . ready to nurse a son,
A version of myself, the infant understood
In the end as the way my own death had come.

Or will I in a decade be back here again,
The diagnosis this time not freakish but fatal?
The changes in one's later years all tend,
Until the last one, toward the farcical,

Each of us slowly turned into something that hurts,
Someone we no longer recognize.
If soul is the final shape I shall assume,

(—*A knock at the door. Time to button my shirt*
And head back out into the waiting room.)
Which of my bodies will have been the best disguise?

1. _____

2. _____

THOU SHALT NOT TAKE THE NAME
3. **OF THE LORD THY GOD IN VAIN** _____

4. _____

5. _____

6. _____

7. _____

8. _____

9. _____

10. _____

Bonhoeffer writes: "Temptation leads us not
Into sin but out of our complacency.
The sins of long ago are suddenly
Alive again, and everything we thought
Behind us. Now we cannot test our powers
But are abandoned by them, or by God.
An honest skeptic's faith is left like a gnawed
Leg in the trap. This is the darkest hour.

Satan knows that what the flesh most fears
Is suffering, and asks, 'Is this what God
Has really said? Who can rely on a word?'
A version of the truth is where the lie appears.
So all temptation is guilt and punishment.
I FALL FROM MYSELF is what the apple meant."

FOUND PARABLE

In the men's room at the office today
some wag has labelled the two stalls
    the *Erotic* and the *Political*.
The second seems suitable for the results
of my business, not for what thinking
    ordinarily accompanies it.
So I've locked myself into the first because,
though farther from the lightbulb overhead,
    it remains the more conventional
and thereby illuminating choice.
The wit on its walls is more desperate.
    As if I had written them
there myself, but only because by now
I have seen them day after day,
    I know each boast, each plea,
the runty widower's resentments,
the phone number for good head.
    Today's fresh drawing:
a woman's torso, neck to outflung knees,
with breasts like targets and at her crotch
    red felt-tip "hair" to guard
a treasure half wound, half wisecrack.
The first critic of the flesh is always
    the self-possessed sensualist.
With all that wall as his margin,
he had sniffed in smug ballpoint
    OBVIOUSLY DONE BY SOMEONE
WHO HAS NEVER SEEN THE REAL THING.
Under that, in a later hand,
    the local pinstripe aesthete

had dismissed the daydreamer's crudity
and its critic's edgy literalism.
    His block letters had squared,
not sloping shoulders: N O,
BY SOMEONE WHO JUST CAN'T DRAW.
    Were the two opinions
converging on the same moral point?
That a good drawing *is* the real thing?
    Or that the real thing
can be truly seen only through another's
eyes? But now that I trace it through
    other jokes and members,
the bottom line leads to a higher inch
of free space on the partition—
    a perch above the loose
remarks, like the pimp's doorway
or the Zen master's cliff-face ledge.
    THERE ARE NO REAL THINGS
writes the philosopher. But he too
has been misled by everything
    the mind makes of a body.
When the torso is fleshed out
and turns over in the artist's bed,
    when the sensualist sobs over her,
when the critic buttons his pants,
when the philosopher's scorn sinks back
    from a gratified ecstasy,
then it will be clear to each
in his own way. There is nothing
    we cannot possibly not know.

MY SIDESHOW

Summers during the Eisenhower years, a carnival
Came to town. From my father's pair of bleacher seats,
The safety net under the Big Top's star attractions,
The drugged tiger, the stilted clowns, the farting scooters
All seemed as little death-defying as those routines
The high-wire trio staged with their jerky parasols.

With that singular lack of shame only a kid commands,
I'd sneak over instead to the sawdusted sideshow tent.
Every year *they* were back: the fire-breathing women,
The men who swallowed scimitars or hammered nails
Up their noses and fishhooks through their tongues,
The dwarf in his rayon jockstrap and sequined sweatband.

A buck got you into the blow-off where a taped grind
Spieled the World of Wonders while a blanket rose
On seven clear ten-gallon jars that held
Pickled fetuses—real or rubber?—their limbs
Like ampersands, each with something deliriously wrong,
Too little of this in front or too much of that behind.

Four-legged chickens, a two-headed raccoon,
The Mule-Faced Girl, the Man with Four Pupils
In His Eyes, coffined devil babies, the Penguin Boy,
The Living Skeleton, an avuncular thousand-pound
Sort who swilled cans of soda and belched at us. . . .
What I think of the Word Made Flesh developed in this
    darkroom.

Back then I couldn't wait for hair to appear on my face
And down below, where my flashlight scrutinized at bedtime.
I'd rise and fall by chance, at the table, on buses, in class.
My voice cracked. I was shooting up and all thumbs.
Oh, the restless embarrassments of late childhood!
My first pimple—huge and lurid—had found its place.

I kept staring at one jar. The thing inside seemed to float
Up from a fishtail that was either leg or penis—or both.
(I could hear my father now, outside the tent, calling me.)
From its mouth, a pair of delicate legs emerged,
As if it had swallowed a perfect twin. I gulped. Something
Unspoken, then and since, rose like acid in my throat.

·

UNDER HYDRA

To disbelieve in God—or worse, in His servants—
    Of old incited mobs
  With stones or stake grimly to atone for what,
    Like a bomb not lobbed
But planted in the garage of a mirror-skin
    High-rise, has from deep within
    Too suddenly exposed
  The common desire to learn
    Less than had been supposed.

Bedsores, point shaving, a taste for sarongs. There are signs
    Everywhere—like the thumbprints,
  Say, of thin-lipped men or sluggish women
    On an heirloom violin.
So mine is the culture of laugh track and chat room.
    Authority's foredoomed.
    Where is distance, and what
  Can frighten or inspire, condemn or redeem?
    All transcendence is cut

With a canned, buttoned-down, fork-tongued coziness.
    The stars are hooded now.
  The heart's cloud chamber weeps its nuclear tears.
    My nails are bitten, and how
All-consuming my vanities, the fancied slights
    To my air-kissing appetites.
    Millennial echoes
  Fill the abandoned stadium. Homeless
    Frauds crowd the two back rows.

Compel them to come in, the evangelist
    Insists. There are empty
  Seats at the table for minims and ranters.
    Join the ancient family
Squabbles—whose is bigger? who deserves more?
    Prophecy's the trapdoor
    Whose fatal saving grace
  Leads to listening for a voice within
    That doubles as self-praise.

His lips cut off, and flames at work on his bubbling guts,
    The wandering monk is tied
  To his own refusal—a book or belief.
    The scholar, for his pride,
Is whipped, branded, and in midwinter sent out
    On the road of his doubt
    To perish of the cold.
  Judge and martyr each invokes God's mercy
    On his innocent soul.

There goes the pitiful procession of mumblers,
    Slave masters and skinheads,
  Witches, dealers, backwoods ayatollahs.
    And here am I, tucked in bed,
Wondering if I believe in anything more
    Than my devotions and four
    Squares. And if forced to say,
  Wouldn't I deny even you, love, for a future?
    Who spoke the truth today?

1. _____

2. _____

3. _____

REMEMBER THAT THOU KEEP
HOLY THE SABBATH DAY

4. _____

5. _____

6. _____

7. _____

8. _____

9. _____

10. _____

That shadow on the wall is looking strange.
A chameleon knows it's easier to change
       Color than to move.

Look at the time! Better just ignore
The threat and stick to a bland esprit de corps,
       Whatever it may prove.

LULLABY

Sleep, my baby,
Sleep your fill.
Sleep, my baby,
Sleep until
The damn birds sing,
Sleep until
The noon bells ring,
Sleep until
The waiters bring
Another round, another bill,
Another night to stand on end.
Sleep the day through,
Sleep the night off.
Sleep it all off, big baby,
Sleep it off again.
And when you wake,
Oh when you wake—
I'll be gone by then, big baby,
I'll be gone by then.

Sleep, old baby,
Sleep your fill.
Sleep, old baby,
Sleep until
The dancers shout,
Sleep until
The stars burn out,
Sleep until
Tonight's boy scout
Gives you a hand, gives you a pill,

Lugs you up the flight of stairs.
Sleep until there's
Nothing more to scare you,
No one left to care,
No one in here,
No one out there,
No one anywhere you are.
Sleep it all off, big baby,
Sleep it off again.
And when you wake,
Oh when you wake—
I'll be gone by then, big baby,
I'll be gone by then.

SOMETIMES

I have sometimes wanted
to stay all night
on a lupine's lip,
a maple's leafgrid
plotting the moonrise,
the stars so close
their beasts and heroes,
locked all along
in the old story,
leave an ashen
dreamspoor behind,
as the night chill
seeps out
of the petal's blue
veins, the spike's
damp streaks,
and keep watch
by the slickered sill
a drowsy bee
stumbles onto
and wait for the dawn
to deal the dark
into glazed shadows
just as a thrush
utters the day's
first will
and testament.

·

I have sometimes wanted
to sit all day
in the hotel bar,
with a damp napkin's
blurred logo,
the lotus incised
around the rim
of my highball
and in the dimmer's
instant twilight
to watch the mirrored
skyline of brands
reflect the row
of laminated awards
from police clubs
or Condé Nast,
the cactus in a beer can
or pear in a bottle,
and on a high shelf
a sawed-off shot glass's
camera obscura
in which to see
myself upturned,
steadied and refilled
with a water back,
everything unnatural,
a companionable solitude.

VARIATIONS ON LINES

CANCELLED BY DICKINSON

Oh Magnanimity—
My Visitor in Paradise—

Sitting on the tiny balcony with another cup of coffee,
The pots of geraniums, the scalloped awning, the cock and
    spire,
I continually imagine myself inside, listening for him.
Boots stamping. His coat smoothed. A knock at the door.

So here is the devil's workshop,
These hands that have held my face,
That cut out palms and horned toads
To paste on the walls of the rain room,
That slowly rubbed both leg stumps,
That separated the pebbles into piles,
That batted a weightless bag of argonite
In the space shuttle's cluttered cockpit,
That cupped a sparrow and let it go,
That finger the change in both pockets,
That deal out doomed games of solitaire,
That trail the fork through a cream sauce
To trace the outlines of a small utopia,
That doodled during an adulterous call,
That oiled the glove, the hinge, the barrel,
These hands that have held my face.

A true story: When the forest fire was finally out
And soldiers scoured the scorched square miles,
They found a body incongruously dressed
In scuba gear—and dead, it was determined,
Not from inhalation but from impact.
Dental records revealed he was a diver
Exploring curiosities on the coastal shelf
Whom a military plane, dispatched to fill itself
With tons of seawater, had inadvertently sucked up,
Flown inland hundreds of miles in its dark hold,
And dropped through a torrent of air onto the flames,
As when great-souled Achilles, gasping for breath,
Having struggled to surface from his grief,
At last puts on his armor, its edges still crusted
With his dead friend's blood, and suddenly charges
Through his own startled ranks toward the river
To slaughter young men and heave their bodies—
Gashed and gorgeous—into the boiling current.

Sunday, July the 4th. Flye Point, Maine.
All morning at the shore, pants rolled up,
Among the trussed skeins of mussels I mean
To make my dinner of. The fog here
Doesn't descend but rather raises the drop
Of common illusion, all color, contrast,
Scale, and vista gone. And how everything
But myself seems concentrated up
Toward someone's finer attention.
The knot garden, say, of an urchin's groining,
Each ridge of delicate bonework receding up
Into the thin air's vanishing point—how at odds
With these tongue-tied rocks at random,
Starfish akimbo, great floes of bladder wrack,
Ruins of demonface shells sucked clean,
The pocked and sizzling marl, then pairs

Of blind eyes the tide's left staring
At their own small lives—and at mine.
Home with a bucket full of meditation
In time for the afternoon spent choosing
Sides at the ballfield, Team Spirit by then
The genius of the shaggy, newly bagged place.
Mouths full of melon and down on all fours,
Babies crawled among the women keeping score.
The resident old bay mare, startled at shortstop,
Moved off to left field, knee-high in wild carrot.
I left before too much had been won or lost.
Then later, the parade. The mayor in her Dodge.
A Minuteman. A heifer. The fife and drum.
Our fire truck, named "Glad Tidings."
A towhead stapled into cardboard
And tugging her squeaky Red Rocket wagon
Full of glossy sawtooth waves and a sign,
"Moon Pulling the Sea Tides." Behind her,
An antinuclear family with their PEACE poster,
His gray-shot beard and serious pothead eyes,
Her bovine sweetness gently switching flies
From their month-old son in his stroller
Wreathed with a strung-out daisy chain.
Their mild dissent is taken in stride,
Part of the rag-tag march of convictions circling
Every town hall in New England today
Where the village orator—ours is Rev. Ezra Fish—
Will summon memories of a miraculous birth:
It was, fellow citizens, a momentous action.
And a true and rightful independence
It remains, to stand before the world and pledge,
As that band of noble men once did on this day,
Each to each and to the common cause,
Our lives, our property, and our sacred honor.
That was surely a most noteworthy day.
If it carried, a new and mighty nation was born.

If not, they swung between heaven and earth. . . .
It ends with a solemn bell, long since melted
Down from cannons, ringing the land's redemption.
No silent, grass-growing calm here but a pine-board
Chariot bearing down on history's phantoms.
Then the crowd scatters in order later to gather
At the baseball field and picture its feelings
In fireworks whose momentary brilliance
Makes the dark more thoroughly dark.
Fat, off-color peonies and lazy mums.
Before *ahhhs* turn to *ummms*, they mount,
Refined to weaving sleek spangled carp
In formation, in turn exploding, whole
Constellations quenched in the harbor
But not before highlighting new myths—
Captain of Industry, Swimming-Hole Gang,
Suffragette Army, Conestoga Wagon Family,
Any surefire standard of self-made men and women
That blacks out in time the pulsing sparks
Of doubt or lust or any wish to be alone
With thoughts that circle the earth like visitors
In paradise, gazing on a night that has gone,
As to the far coast of home, so gloriously forth.

1. _____

2. _____

3. _____

4. _____

HONOR THY FATHER
AND THY MOTHER

5. _____

6. _____

7. _____

8. _____

9. _____

10. _____

In Milgram's famous experiment at Yale,
The "teacher" was told the study concerned the effects
Of punishment on learning, and instructed to send
An electric shock to the "student" whenever he made
A wrong answer, the voltage level and the pain
Set to increase automatically, from SLIGHT
To (thirty switches further on) SEVERE.
The scientist would determine when he's through.

The "student," of course, is an actor and coached to fail.
The shocks continue. At first he looks perplexed,
Then grunts, complains, protests, and, in the end,
Screams to be spared. The "teacher" hesitates.
You're helping science, the Higher Authority explains.
Ordered to go on and released from his moral plight,
He pushes the button again. It's as we feared:
People will do what they are told to do.

Through the peephole he could see a boy
Playing patience on the huge crimson sofa.
    There was the carpet, the second-best
Chairs, the old chipped washstand, all his dead parents'
        Things donated months ago
        "To make an unfortunate
    Crowd happy" at the Hôtel
    Marigny, Albert's brothel,
Warehouse of desires
And useless fictions—

For one of which he turned to Albert
And nodded, he'd have that one at cards, the soon-
    To-be footman or fancy butcher.
He'd rehearsed his questions in the corridor.
        Did you kill an animal
        Today? An ox? Did it bleed?
        Did you touch the blood? Show me
        Your hands, let me see how you . . .
(Judgment Day angel
Here to separate

The Good from the Bad, to weigh the soul . . .
Soon enough you'll fall from grace and be nicknamed
    Pamela the Enchantress or Tool
Of the Trade. Silliness is the soul's sweetmeat.)
        One after another now,
        Doors closed on men in bed with
    The past, it was three flights to
    His room, the bedroom at last,
The goal obtained and
So a starting point

For the next forbidden fruit—the taste
Of apricots and ripe gruyère is on the hand
He licks—the next wide-open mouth
To slip his tongue into like a communion
Wafer. The consolation
Of martyrs is that the God
For whom they suffer will see
Their wounds, their wildernesses.
He's pulled a fresh sheet
Up over himself,

As if waiting for his goodnight kiss
While the naked boy performs what he once did
For himself. It's only suffering
Can make us all more than brutes, the way that boy
Suffers the silvery thread
To be spun inside himself,
The snail track left on lilac,
Its lustrous mirror-writing,
The mysterious
Laws drawn through our lives

Like a mother's hand through her son's hair . . .
But again nothing comes of it. The signal
Must be given, the small bedside bell.
He needs his parents to engender himself,
To worship his own body
As he watches them adore
Each other's. The two cages
Are brought in like the holy
Sacrament. Slowly
The boy unveils them.

The votive gaslights seem to flicker.
Her dying words were "What have you done to me?"
    In each cage a rat, and each rat starved
For three days, each rat furiously circling
        The pain of its own hunger.
        Side by side the two cages
      Are placed on the bed, the foot
      Of the bed, right on the sheet
Where he can see them
Down the length of his

    Body, helpless now as it waits there.
The rats' angry squealing sounds so far away.
    He looks up at his mother—touches
Himself—at her photograph on the dresser,
        His mother in her choker
        And her heavy silver frame.
      The tiny wire-mesh trapdoors
      Slide open. At once the rats
Leap at each other,
Claws, teeth, the little

    Shrieks, the flesh torn, torn desperately,
Blood spurting out everywhere, hair matted, eyes
    Blinded with the blood. Whichever stops
To eat is further torn. The half-eaten rat
        Left alive in the silver
        Cage the boy—he keeps touching
      Himself—will stick over and
      Over with a long hatpin.
Between his fingers
He holds the pearl drop.

    She leans down over the bed, her veil
Half-lifted, the scent of lilac on her glove.
    His father hates her coming to him
Like this, hates her kissing him at night like this.

PANTOUM

Who doesn't need an evil parent
To explain why the world doesn't love us
From the start, why the heart's unjust,
Why happiness is veiled like a widow?

To explain why the world doesn't love her,
Pamina's handed a dagger by her mother
Whose happiness is veiled like a widow's,
Cutthroat stars disguised as tears.

Pamina's handed the dagger by her mother,
The frigid Queen of the Night
Whose cutthroat stars are disguised as tears,
Then told how the days abandoned her.

The frigid Queen of the Night
Had long since betrayed her true victim
By telling her the days had abandoned her,
The lie in the voice half-choked with fear.

Himself once betrayed, her intended victim
Tries to give his daughter life again.
The lie in the voice half-choked with fear
That sings on and on in the blood—

He wants to warn his daughter it will try again.
He wants to tell her to love herself alone.
What sings on and on in the blood
Is the body's shrill familiar chaos.

He wants to teach her how to love herself alone.
But she isn't listening to reason, and never will.
The body's sullen familiar chaos
Lights her way to its moonlit marriage bed.

She isn't listening to reason, and never will.
Who doesn't need an evil parent
To light the way to a moonlit marriage bed?
From the start, the heart is unjust.

TEA WITH THE

LOCAL SAINT

For Jane Garmey

I'd bought a cone of solid sugar and a box
Of tea for the saint himself, a flashlight
For his son, the saint-elect, and bubblegum
For a confusion of small fry—the five-year-old
Aunt, say, and her seven-year-old nephew.
Nothing for the women, of course, the tattooed,
One-eyed, moon-faced matron, or her daughter
Whose husband had long ago run away
After killing their newborn by pouring
A bottle of cheap cologne down its throat.
This was, after all, our first meeting.

I was to be introduced by a Peace Corps pal
Whose easy, open California ways
Had brought a water system to the village
And an up-to-date word to its vocabulary.
Every other guttural spillway of Arabic
Included a carefully enunciated "awesome,"
The speaker bright-eyed with his own banter.
We sat on a pair of Kurt Cobain beach towels
And under a High-Quality Quartz Clock,
The plastic butterflies attached to whose hands
Seemed to keep time with those in my stomach.

At last, he entered the room, the saint himself,
Moulay Madani, in a white head scarf and caftan
The fading blue of a map's Moroccan coastline,

Its hem embroidered with geometric ports of call.
A rugged sixty, with a longshoreman's jaw,
A courtier's guile, and a statesman's earnest pauses,
He first explained the crescent dagger he fingered
Had been made two centuries ago by a clever Jew.
Then he squinted for my reaction. I've no taste
For bad blood, and gingerly cleared my throat to say
I was inclined to trust any saint who carried a knife.

From a copper urn, glasses of mint tea were poured,
Of a tongue-stiffening sweetness. I was allowed to wave
Away the tray of nougat—or rather, the flies on it.
Sipping, I waited for a word, a sign from the saint.
I'd wanted to lie, as if underground, and watch
Him dig up the sky, or stand at a riverbank
And have the water sweep off my presumptions,
Have him blow light into my changeling bones.
I wanted to feel the stalk rise and the blade fall.
I wanted my life's arithmetic glazed and fired.
I wanted the hush, the wingstroke, the shudder.

But sainthood, I learned soon enough, is a fate
Worse than life, nights on call for the demons
In a vomiting lamb, a dry breast, a broken radio,
And days spent parroting the timeless adages,
Spent arbitrating water rights, property lines,
Or feuds between rival herdsmen over scrub brush,
Spent blessing every bride and anyone's big-bellied
Fourth or fifth wife, praying that they deliver sons.
I thought back to the time, not ten feet from him,
I heard a homily delivered by old John XXIII,
Sounding wholly seraphic in his murmured Italian.

Ten interpreters stepped from behind the throne.
The English one at last explained the Holy Father
Had urged us all to wear seatbelts while driving.

My heart sank at its plain good sense, as hymns
Echoed and golden canopies enfolded the pope.
How like home it seemed, with my own father
A preoccupied patriarch of practicality
When what was wanted veered wildly between
The gruff headmaster and the drunken playwright.
Instead, I got the distant advertising salesman,
The suburban dad of what turned out to be my dreams. . . .

Dreams that, decades later, back at my hotel in Fez,
A bucket of cold water was suddenly poured on.
I'd gone to the hammam, stripped, and lay on a pattern
Of sopping tiles that might have spelled God's will.
Steam shrouded the attendant methodically soaping
The knots of disappointment he'd knuckled in my back.
He paused. I drifted. [*The freezing shock.*] I looked up
At a bald, toothless gnome in swaddling clothes
On his way back to the fountain for more bad news.
Something in his bowlegged walk—perhaps the weary
Routine of it—made me think of the saint again,

Of how, when tea was done, and everyone had stood,
He reached for my head, put his hands over it,
And gently pulled me to his chest, which smelled
Of dung smoke and cinnamon and mutton grease.
I could hear his wheezy breathing now, like the prophet's
Last whispered word repeated by the faithful.
Then he prayed for what no one had time to translate—
His son interrupted the old man to tell him a group
Of snake charmers sought his blessing, and a blind thief.
The saint pushed me away, took one long look,
Then straightened my collar and nodded me toward the
    door.

1. _____

2. _____

3. _____

4. _____

5. _____

6. **THOU SHALT DO NO MURDER** _____

7. _____

8. _____

9. _____

10. _____

There would be no need to prohibit
What no one desires to do.
Though conscience may inhibit,
Says Totem and Taboo,

Our parents, kings, and priests
Rouse a fierce temptation.
A proper horror's increased
By the mess of motivation.

BODIES

It's not the life but the body
That fascinates after the fact.
When one head was brought to Nero
He joked about its premature
Grayness. Of another he wondered aloud why
Long noses once frightened him.
After he ordered poison for his mother
Staff officers doubled their gaming bets.
On temple walls these were the thank-offerings:
Orators' tongues, a commander's feet,
The empress's hands, with all their rings.
Bodies give up their secrets.

At parties he introduced a new entertainment.
Dressed in wild animal skins,
He was released from a jewelled cage
And attacked the private parts
Of husbands and wives bound to stakes
Until slaves ceremonially "slaughtered" him.

How next to kill the recurring dream?
He is steering a ship
But a corpse tears the tiller
From his hands while winged ants
Swarm over him and huge statues prevent
His escape. No, his horse!
But once mounted, the horse turns into
An ape, except the head,
Which brays something like a lyre tune
He once played at festivals.
Animals! Their mouths, their smell, their meat.
It's animals that betrayed us.

SNIPER

The geedee cannon cockers with their illumes
And boom-boom arty always miss the point.
It's not just they're too late to hit Charlie
In his hooch or shake him from the palm trees.
The hot dogs who lug the stuff by elephant
From Laos, down the trail to Duc Pho,
All the way from the Kremlin to some old granny's
Thatched hut, under the baby's cradle,
They're like raindrops out here—you ignore
The soaker and wipe the single ones away.

The spotter's laid his greasepaint on so thick
The geckos' tails are quivering. A sniper
Doesn't care. Your heart's in the mulch beneath
Your chest, your arm the glass-bedded stock and floating
Barrel, your eye the long Unertl scope
On a match-conditioned Model-70 Winchester.
You lie there dead-on and never think of home,
Of razorbacks or sweet potato pie.
You think of fifteen hundred yards ahead.
Red Man, Red Man. Evil Eye three-six.

A bicycle, with four Kalashnikovs
Slung to its handlebars, three more tied
Beneath the seat with haversacks of cartridges
In bandoleers or hook-nosed magazines.
Your trigger finger tightens. But in the cross hairs
The mule's a twelve-year-old. You have a clean shot,
So you send a heavy boat-tailed bullet
Into the front wheel. The boy is thrown wide,

The cargo scattered. Why do rice-paddy gooners
Send their kids to do the work of death?

You have the chance at last to teach a lesson
By sending him back to school, but the kid has scrambled
To an automatic and, like it's a firefight, has jammed
A clip in. You don't think again, not even
Of the snuffies back in camp all this ammo's
Meant to zip up into bodybags. You drop him.
You'd do it again, even as you watch him kick
In the dirt, the wheels still slowly turning.
The spotter's bugged, but you explain they flop
Around a lot when you shoot them in the head.

FLIES

The agent, years ago in Argentina,
watched through a metal eyelet
in the tarpaulin as Eichmann
bought his newspaper at the kiosk.

In his report he noted the old man's
average height, bald head, large nose,
mustache, glasses, pressed tan trousers,
gray overcoat, patternless green tie.

He did not enter through the front gate
but bent under a wire marking the side
boundary of his plot and walked slowly
across the yard. A child ran up to him.

The agent couldn't see clearly. Cars went by.
The man had been leaning over,
whispering to the boy, and seemed
to be gently stroking his face,

then climbed the steps to the porch,
brushing away flies with the newspaper.
The agent felt something brush against
his face. He was about to open the door

when a stocky woman in a housecoat
opened it from inside. As he walked in,
they both absently waved to keep
the flies away from the open door.

1. _____

2. _____

3. _____

4. _____

5. _____

6. _____

7. THOU SHALT NOT COMMIT ADULTERY _____

8. _____

9. _____

10. _____

Whatever dreams of escape may cast their spell,
From a tiny room inside the Buddha's topknot
Your double rings a faint instinctive bell:
taste touch sight sound smell

Now that sex is "safe" and you're still "well,"
You think that thinking is the cause of "sin"?
The fatal warning's imprinted on each cell:
taste touch sight sound smell

You run your hand along his thigh and tell
Him bourgeois culture's still a liberal plot.
The oppressor's pride at once begins to swell:
taste touch sight sound smell

To avoid desire, the Chinese sages dwell
In Nothing they've cut doors and windows in.
For all their bark, the straw dogs bite as well:
taste touch sight sound smell

The body of knowledge, stuck in a book-lined hell,
Twists on a wick of grief. In flames not hot
But burning hard it takes from flesh its farewell:
taste touch sight sound smell

CHOTT

Through the tent flap, across the air mattress, up over my
  shoulderblade,
The bandage of sunlight slips into place. On your borrowed
  Walkman

The muezzin's morning call to prayer clears its throat of
  unbelief.
Already out there pillars of sand are forming to hold up
  the sky

For minutes at a time before they buckle and collapse with
  exhaustion.
One more day on the salt flats. Air tight as a water-skin.
  Black flies

On your eyelid. Sun. Two suns, the counterfeit sun curling
  like a petal,
Separating from the true, wrenched from it to simmer on its
  reflection,

A hand's breadth between them now, the true one hauled up
  dripping.
Whose idea was a week on a dead sea anyway? A week away
  from the port,

Away from the café's chewed pits and prawnshuck, the
  feather-edged kef.
In their teaching rooms, the holy men were promising *He has
  forced*

The night and the day into your service, set forgiving mountains down
Lest the earth should move away with you. Caked mud and brine
crust,

Like two drops of blood on a pillow, both dried to the same
charred brick.
To reach for the newspaper risks touching you. The Jeep
hood flutters.

Out beyond your head, slumped now over your breasts, the
horizon's
Hit on the day's first mirage—lolling palms, a milky water
hole,

Two Frenchmen in rockers. Is that a woman, her arm up to
shade her eyes?
Or protect herself? A bronze basin over—(*Wake up, damn you!*
Wake. Up.)

A mirage, the goatherd said, is always something you once
had or wanted.
So by that logic, the past . . . no matter. It was only another
promise.

Remember those first days in bed? The braided candlelight,
the net of stars,
The shadow-drawn streams running underneath the body,
under the loathing.

The years, the miles out and back are run through us, just
sitting here.
This whole thing, it's inside a bottle, that empty fifth
Hussein kept

His miniature desert in for the tourists, the dwarfed ruins
    he'd tweezered
Onto a dirty inch of nowhere, the how many layers of
    wornaway rock,

The grains of lives dry as the world's bone. Look at the sun
    in there,
That glistening drop of poison at the tip of the scorpion's
    tail.

The room with double beds, side by side.
One was the bed of roses, still made up,
The other the bed of nails, all undone.
In the nightstand clamshell, two Marlboro butts.

On the shag, a condom with a tear in its tip
Neither of them noticed—or would even suspect
For two years more. A ballpoint embossed
By a client's firm: Malpractice Suits.

A wad of gum balled in a page of proverbs
Torn from the complimentary Bible.
His lipstick. Her aftershave.

A dream they found the next day they'd shared:
All the dogs on the island were dying
And the birds had flown up into the lonely air.

THE DIALOGUE OF DESIRE
AND GUILT

Even I want
The adulterer's thrilled
Panic—the night away, the night back home.
I want to stay hard and have it both ways,
Deaf to the heart's dull drill
And love's cheap taunt.

Odds are someone's household gods will oblige.
But how much of romance
Is mere relief?
The sound you think
Of as longing's sigh
Finally comes clear as the moan of regret.

The first desire
Is to feel that one is
Desired, not just called on but called for.
I need the hindrance, too—spouse or scruple,
A slight deformity,
A barking dog.

The last laugh is your arrogant demand
That the world change into
Your wish for it.
Go make a meal—
Chipped beef on burnt toast points?—
Of your old quarrel with the Devouring Mom.

The most I can
Offer—my final bid,
Let's say—is a couple of weeks, perhaps
A month. I'm all yours. I'll eat and drink you,
Wake and dream you, make you
Want what I want.

The least of it is wanting. Flatterers
Around a stuttering
Tyrant always
Try to guess what
He is about to say,
Even mouth their own sudden banishment.

Everything's called
By a secret name, pulled
On silken threads across the eye's instant.
Let me put my hand just inside the wound,
So warm and familiar.
The flesh is home.

Nothing helps. The cloudy consolations,
The zigzag alibis,
The sodden ache
To be alone.
Look up at the night sky.
It's time to swallow the storm's bitter pearl.

1. _____

2. _____

3. _____

4. _____

5. _____

6. _____

7. _____

8. THOU SHALT NOT STEAL _____

9. _____

10. _____

Jacob bought a birthright
From his starving older twin
With a common pot of lentils.
And a sympathetic grin.

Next he tricked a blessing
From his blind and dying father
Who felt the one's disguise
And mistook him for the other.

Touching his head to the ground,
His fortunes by then reversed,
In Esau years later he found

A patience that made things worse:
Forgiveness brought him down.
What he'd claimed in the end was a curse.

AFTER OVID

APOLLO AND HYACINTHUS

Guilt's dirty hands, memory's kitchen sink . . .
    It's bad faith makes immortal love.
        Take a closer look at Hyacinth.

Dark bud-tight curls and poppy-seed stubble,
    The skin over his cheekbones pale as poison
        Slowly dripped from eye to eye,

And a crotch that whispers its single secret
    Even from behind the waiter's apron.
        He's sulking now, staring at the traffic.

Every year there's a new one at the bar
    Sprung from whatever nowhere—the country,
        The islands, the Midwest . . .

The old man at the far corner table, decades ago
    Called by his critics "the sun god
        Of our poetry," sits stirring

A third coffee and an opening line,
    Something like *So often you renew*
        Yourself or *You and I resemble*

Nothing else *Every other pair of lovers.*
        The grease stain on his left sleeve
            Winks as the lights come on.

He signals the boy and means to ask
        Under cover of settling the check
            If, with the usual understanding

And for the same pleasures, he'd return again
        Tonight, after work, there was something
            He'd wanted to show the boy, a picture

Of two sailors that if held upside down . . .
        It's then he notices the gold cufflinks
            The boy is wearing, the pair the poet's

Friends had given him when his first book—
        That moist sheaf of stifled longings—
            Appeared to doting acclaim.

To have stolen from one who would give
        Anything: what better pretext
            To put an end to "an arrangement"?

The old man falls silent, gets up from his seat,
        Leaves a few coins on the table,
            And walks out through his confusions,

Homeward through the side streets, across the square,
        Up the fifty-two stone steps, up the years
            And back to his study, its iron cot.

The heaving had stopped. The last sad strokes
        Of the town clock had rung: Anger was one,
            Humiliation the other.

He sat there until dawn and wrote out the poem
      That has come to be in all the anthologies,
         The one you know, beginning

You are my sorrow and my fault. The one that goes
      In all my songs, in my mind, in my mouth,
         The sighing still sounds of you.

The one that ends with the boy—the common,
      Adored, two-timing hustler—turned
         Into a flower, *the soft-fleshed lily*

But of a blotched purple that grief will come
      To scar with its initials A I, A I.
         O, the ache insists.

STOLEN HOURS

The day with T—an arrow
    drawn from the quiver
still so filled with sharp regrets.

     •

  I lied to the boss.
Mother wasn't sick at all.
    But next month she died.

     •

My hour with C. I'm the thief
    who swallows the jewel
while making his quick escape.

     •

    That house in Mystic
written off as an expense?
    Yes, the cost of light.

     •

ATMs, the microwave,
    the damn VCR . . .
high-tech schemes for time with you.

     •

    Two chapters at night.
A movie during the day.
    Oh, the sex between!

     •

These mornings in the garden:
    what exactly is
being planted, watered, grown?

                    •

The door closed, the phone turned off,
    feet up on the desk—
the bureaucratic sublime!

                    •

    The thousand glimpses—
do they add up to a life
    seen sideways, seen right?

                    •

What a relief that
official thievery thrives:
    Daylight Savings Time.

                    •

Never having to explain
    a mood or motive
saves those weekends with old friends.

                    •

    Last year's overtime,
idly now recalled, led to
    my nervous breakthrough.

                    •

The late light stays on the trees,
in the leaves: autumn
moving now across the hill.

.

This noise at daybreak:
the trashmen busy outside
hauling the night off.

AFTER MAGRITTE

The sill is clammy to the touch, and the view familiar.
But doesn't that moon seem a little *too* familiar?

His severed hand had been in someone's pocket.
The stars hang perilously above Rue Familiar.

The whore's pigeons seemed safe under his bowler,
But when he spotted an opening, the banker grew familiar.

His cloud saddle strapped to the sky's flanks,
The Liberator arrived out of the blue. Familiar

Ideas, like glass shards, lay all over the floor,
Each with a part of the field pasted to familiar

Problems from the front page—the war, the scandals.
Men in uniform left us free to pursue familiar

Desires. But which came first, the cage or the egg?
What you dreamt was overdue, what you knew familiar.

Who owns the light? Who sold the sea its waves?
Perspective is the devil's new familiar.

If all property is theft, nothing's left to give
The old man in Brussels but a few familiar

Imitations on cheap posters, enough to make seem
Strange what delicacies had been hitherto familiar.

Here is the pearl that made a grain of sand,
And the bricked-up alphabet that made you familiar.

1. _____

2. _____

3. _____

4. _____

5. _____

6. _____

7. _____

8. _____

9. THOU SHALT NOT BEAR
   FALSE WITNESS _____

10. _____

"Why should we not do evil then,"
  The letter continued, self-satisfied,
"That good may come of it for all?"

  A fair question, the apostle replied,
  And one that troubles better men.
  But can the good be everyone's fault?

"Put away lying and speak the truth,"
  He urged, "each one with his neighbor
  Because we are members of one another."
  The withered limb, the half-blind eye . . .

  Each results from who'd say more
  Or less than is enough to prove—
  Despite the tic or wink or stutter—
  The lies that bind are all untied.

HONEST IAGO

If ever I did dream of such a matter,
Abhor me. And remember, I know my place.
In following him, I follow but myself.
    All I want to do is help.

I'd rather have the tongue cut from my mouth
Than speak against my friend. This crack of love
Will grow stronger than it ever was before.
    There's reason to cool our raging, no?

I cannot think he means to do you any harm.
The chemotherapy seems promising.
These latest figures will show you what I mean.
    All I want to do is help.

I had not thought he was acquainted with her.
Yes, yes, this boxcar is returning to Poland.
Sure, I've already tested negative twice.
    I am bound to every act of duty.

Your sins are forgiven. This is only a phase.
I could swear it was her handkerchief I saw.
Trust me. Everything is under control.
    All I want to do is help.

in the old oxblood edition, the color
　　of the mother tongue, all foxed and forked,
its threadbare edges dented, once a fixture
　　in the second-story Kirchstetten
room where day by day he fashioned the silence
　　into objects, often sitting on
Poy-Ry, say, or *Sole-Sz,* and after his death
　　sent packing from cozy Austria
to Athens, where fortune dropped it from Chester's
　　trembling hands into a legacy
that exiled it next to page-curling Key West
　　and finally to Connecticut,
is shelved here now, a long arm's-length from my desk.
　　What he made of himself he had found
in this book, the exact weight of each soft spot
　　and sore point, how each casts a shadow
understudying our hungers and our whims.
　　If history is just plain dull facts,
the facts are these, these ruling nouns and upstart
　　verbs, these slick adjectival toadies
and adverbial agents with their collars
　　pulled up, privileged phrasal moments,
and full-scale clausal changes that qualify
　　or contradict the course of a life.
This book is all we can remember and dream.
　　It's how spur gears mesh and rocks are parsed
into geodes, how the blood engorges
　　a glance, how the fig ripens to fall,
or what quarter-tones and quarks may signal deep
　　inside a precise idea of space.
It is to this book he sat for the lessons

the past had set him—how our Greeks died,
whom your Romans killed, how her Germans
    overreached, what his English understood,
how my Americans denied history
    was anything but an innocence
the others had simply skimmed or mispronounced.
    He knew history is a grammar,
and grammar a metaphor, and poetry
    nothing more or less than death itself—
it never lies because it never affirms.
    From the start, squinting at the propped score
with Mother in their duets at the upright
    or biting his nails while arguing
the quidditas of thuggish jacks-in-office,
    he knew what he called truth always lies
in the words and so in this dictionary,
    which like him has become a conscience
with all its roots, all its ramifications,
    meanings and examples down the years.
It was on this book he sat for the lessons
    learned five inches above a desk chair,
five inches to lean down closer to the page,
    one volume at a time, day by day,
slightly above the sense of things, but closer
    to what tomorrow so many others
will consider to have somehow been the truth.

The hard part is not so much telling the truth
    as knowing which truth to tell—or worse,
what it is you want to tell the truth, and how
    at last one learns to unlove others,
to uncast the spells, to rewind the romance
    back to its original desire
for something else altogether, its grievance,
    say, against that year's dazzling head boy

or the crippled wide-eyed horse you couldn't shoot.
    And, as innocent as the future
porno star's first milk tooth, the dictionary
    has no morality other than
definition itself. The large, functional
    Indo-European family
will do for a murky myth of origin,
    and the iron laws of shift and change
go unquestioned by the puzzled rummager.
    Our names for things tend to hold them fast
in place, give an X its features or its pitch,
    a fourth dimension of distinctness.
And what may seem vague awaits the Supplement
    just now pulling into the depot,
late as usual but looming through the steam.
    Words have their unflappable habits
of being, constellations of fixed ideas
    that still move. Sentimentality,
Snobbery, Sympathy, Sorrow—each queues up
    at the same window. No raised eyebrow
for the faked orgasm or press conference
    to issue official denials.
No sigh for the botanist's crabbed notebook.
    No praise for the florilegium.
No regret for the sinking tanker's oil slick
    glittering now off Cape Flattery.
No truck with bandbox grooming, fashion runways,
    the foot binder's stale apology,
or the dream's down payment and layaway plan.
    Everything adds up to or sinks back
into the word we know it by in this book.
    A believer in words—common prayers
or textbook theories—this wrinkled metaphor
    of the mind itself abided by
what grave and lucid laws, what keen exemptions
    these columns of small print have upheld.

He could be sitting beside one, chin in hand,
        listening to a late quartet, a gaze
on his face only the final chord will break.
        Here is that faraway something else,
here between the crowded lines of scholarship.
        Here is the first rapture and final
dread of being found out by words, terms, phrases
        for what is unknown, unfelt, unloved.
Here in the end is the language of a life.

Half my life ago, before retiring
        to new digs under Oxford's old spires,
as a part of his farewell tour of the States,
        one last look at the rooms of the house
he'd made of our poised, mechanical largesse,
        he visited my alma mater.
The crowd—tweedy townies and student groundlings—
        packed the hall and spilled over the lawn
outside, where the lucky ones pressed their faces
        to windows suspense was steaming up.
How did I find a place at the master's feet?
        My view was of the great man's ankles,
and close enough to see his socks didn't match.
        I sat there uncomfortably but spellbound
to his oracular mumble. And later,
        after the applause and the sherry,
while he wambled tipsily toward his guest suite,
        I sprang as if by coincidence
from its darkened doorway where I'd been waiting.
        But, well, waiting for *what* exactly?
Suddenly speechless, I counted on a lie
        and told him I knew his work by heart
and would he autograph my unread copy.
        He reached in his jacket for a pen
and at last looked distractedly up at me.

A pause. "Turn around and bend over,"
he ordered in a voice vexed with impatience
    I at once mistook for genuine
interest—almost a proposition, in fact.
    The coy young man I was then is not
my type, but I can recognize the appeal.
    Even as I wheeled slowly around
and put my hands on my knees, I realized
    what he wanted, what he'd asked of me.
To write in the book, he required a desk.
    My back would do as well as any
Tree trunk or cafeteria tabletop.
    Only years later did it make sense.
By then I'd figured out that he'd been writing
    on me ever since that encounter,
or that I'd unconsciously made of myself
    a desk so that he could continue—
the common imagination's dogsbody
    and ringmaster—still to speak up,
however halting or indirect the voice.

Today, sitting down at six to darn the day
    with a drink, I glanced across the room
to my desk, where Wystan, my month-old tabby,
    lay asleep on an open volume
of the wizard's unfailing dictionary,
    faultless creaturely Instinct atwitch
on a monument. How to sneak out past him
    for the sweating martini shaker?
My clumsy tiptoe prompts a faint annoyance—
    a single eye unlidded, a yawn,
his right paw, claws outstretched, pointing to *soodle*.
    Weren't these—the cat and book, or instinct
and idea—the two angels on his shoulder?

Together, they'd made him suspicious
of the holy crusade, the top of the charts,
    compulsive hygiene, debt, middlemen,
seaside cottages, crooners, Gallic charm,
    public charities, the forgeries
of statecraft, the fantasies of the bedroom,
    easy assumptions, and sweeping views.
The kitten's claws have somehow caught in the page
    and puckered it so that, skewed sideways,
it resembles—or rather, for the moment
    I can make out in the lines of type—
the too often folded map his face looked like.
    Protect me, St. Wiz, protect us all
from this century by your true example.
    With what our language has come to know
about us, protect us still from both how much
    and how little we can understand
ourselves, from the unutterable blank page
    of soul, from the echoing silence
moments after the heavy book is slammed shut.

DESCARTES' DREAM

He felt a sudden weakness on his right side
And leaned over to his left to walk the streets
But, sensing he made a foolish figure, straightened up
Only to be spun around by a violent wind
And, as he sought shelter in the college chapel,
Rushed by a man in black he thought he'd known.
Who learns to doubt everything can see
The world's painted dropcloth drawn on strings
Past the grimy window of a *train de vie*.
I will my arm to move but the flesh abides.

Clockmaker, coolie, collaborator—
He will depend on nothing, not the servant
Girl with her small breasts, not the duke's
Armies or the thrumming wheel of logic.
In the quadrangle the others all stood upright
Talking with the friend he'd slighted.
Friend? Whom to trust and whom to shun?
Sudden thunder. Fiery sparks are streaming
Through the room. They come from the friend's mouth.
Truth is whatever darkness we choose to ignore.

He opened the book he found on an upper shelf.
Old tags he recognized but couldn't name.
Someone called to him from the quadrangle.
If he wished to find his friend, here was a gift
To give him, he said, and held out a curious melon,
The seeded song of nature, its germs of light.
He wanted to show the book now to the man,
But as he turned the pages the words slid

Into tiny portraits, copperplate engravings
Of the servant girl, the duke, his mother, himself.

Bodies, those false witnesses, serve the light,
Which would not shine unless it broke against them.
The weight of the falling planet presses into
His eyelids. Suddenly, both the man and the book
Disappeared. The weight lifted. Reason
Again held the reins of the bolting blood-horse.
How far must we get away from the earth to see it
Properly? How long must we go without knowing
Before we discover that everything leads back
To something as simple and dreadful as the night?

1. _____

2. _____

3. _____

4. _____

5. _____

6. _____

7. _____

8. _____

9. _____

10. THOU SHALT NOT COVET _____

Love is injustice, said Camus.
We want to be loved. What's still more true?
Each wants most to be preferred,
And listens for those redeeming words
Better than X, more than Y—
Enough to quiet the child's cry,
The bridegroom's nerves, the patient's
Reluctant belief in providence.
Break what you can, hurt whom you will,
Humiliate the others until
Someone takes a long, hard look.
Oh Love, put down your balance book.

SLAVE SONG

He is my rock and my hiding place
in the time of trials. My brother
he got over to the Northern side.
He walked on water. Doctor Jesus.
The Lord carried him who raises
up those that cry unto heaven.
He outrides any man's ideas,
plants His footsteps on the North,
the South, the East, the West.
Even now he tends my mother
who washed her robes and made them
white in the blood of the Lamb.

First Caesar King was killed
for biting off the overseer's ear.
We cared for his bones and put them
out in the sun in bright weather,
back in a box when it rained.
He knew my father, my white father,
saw him ride in a carriage once,
a great planter who never whipped
his slaves and gave them spoons,
real spoons, not oyster shells.
At hog-killing times it's said
he ate a liver right in the bed of coals.

My mother's slave husband was sold
so the young master could buy a poor
white man to do his army service.
Bloodhounds and nigger-catchers
are neither bond nor free, not one

in Christ Jesus. Weary of my life
I have watched them moor a man up
and lick him so as dogs or cattle
were never flogged, so each of us
could see our own lot if we tried
to run from the vendue, from the day
you're knocked down to a bidder.

I am worth three hundred dollars now.
I have been turned around slowly
in the square, surrounded by men.
My back is smooth as a sorrowing cheek.
I have seen poor Hetty's flesh
raw with licks. The men would rest
an hour, then beat her again,
so she was brought early to bed
and was delivered of a dead child.
She lay on a mat in the kitchen,
her body swelling till the water
burst out of her body and she died.

I have been turned around slowly
in the square. The men have handled
and examined me as butchers will
a calf in the stall. When I came
to this house, the upstairs women
asked who I belonged to. "I am
come to live here," I replied.
"Poor child, poor child,"
they both said over and over.
And I went outside and looked up
to see what would direct me.
I saw a clear space in the sky.

THREE DREAMS

ABOUT ELIZABETH BISHOP

I .

It turned out the funeral had been delayed a year.
The casket now stood in the state capitol rotunda,
An open casket. You lay there like Lenin
Under glass, powdered, in powder blue
But crestfallen, if that's the word
For those sagging muscles that make the dead
Look grumpy. The room smelled of gardenias.
Or no, I *was* a gardenia, part of a wreath
Sent by the Radcliffe Institute and right behind
You, with a view down the line of mourners.
When Lloyd and Frank arrived, both of them
Weeping and reciting—was it "Thanatopsis"?—
A line from Frank about being the brother
To a sluggish clod was enough to wake you up.
One eye, then the other, slowly opened.
You didn't say anything, didn't have to.
You just blinked, or I did, and in another room
A group of us sat around your coffin chatting.
Once in a while you would add a comment—
That, no, hay was stacked with beaverslides,
And, yes, it was a blue, a mimeograph blue
Powder the Indians used, and stuck cedar pegs
Through their breasts in the ghost dance—
All this very slowly. Such an effort for you
To speak, as if underwater and each bubble-
Syllable had to be exhaled, leisurely

Floated up to the surface of our patience.
Still alive, days later, still laid out
In a party dress prinked with sun sparks,
Hands folded demurely across your stomach,
You lay on the back lawn, uncoffined,
Surrounded by beds of freckled foxglove
And fool-the-eye lilies that only last a day.
By then Lowell had arrived, young again
But shaggy even in his seersucker and tie.
He lay down alongside you to talk.
The pleasure of it showed in your eyes,
Widening, then fluttering with the gossip,
Though, of course, you still didn't move at all,
Just your lips, and Lowell would lean in
To listen, his ear right next to your mouth,
Then look up smiling and roll over to tell me
What you said, that since you'd passed over
You'd heard why women live longer than men—
Because they wear big diamond rings.

I I .

She is sitting three pews ahead of me
At the Methodist church on Wilshire Boulevard.
I can make out one maple leaf earring
Through the upswept fog bank of her hair
—Suddenly snapped back, to stay awake.
A minister is lamenting the forgetfulness
Of the laws, and warms to his fable
About the wild oryx, "which the Egyptians
Say stands full against the Dog Star
When it rises, looks wistfully upon it,
And testifies after a sort by sneezing,
A kind of worship but a miserable knowledge."
He is wearing, now I look, the other earring,

Which catches a bluish light from the window
Behind him, palm trees bent in stained glass
Over a manger scene. The Joseph sports
A three-piece suit, fedora in hand.
Mary, in a leather jacket, is kneeling.
The gnarled lead joinder soldered behind
Gives her a bun, protruding from which
Two shafts of a halo look like chopsticks.
Intent on her task, her mouth full of pins,
She seems to be taking them out, one by one,
To fasten or fit with stars the night sky
Over the child's crib, which itself resembles
A Studebaker my parents owned after the war,
The model called an Oryx, which once took
The three of us on the flight into California.
I remember, leaving town one Sunday morning,
We passed a dwarfish, gray-haired woman
Sitting cross-legged on an iron porch chair
In red slacks and a white sleeveless blouse,
A cigarette in her hand but in a silver holder,
Watching us leave, angel or executioner,
Not caring which, pursuing her own thoughts.

I I I .

Dawn through a slider to the redwood deck.
Two mugs on the rail with a trace
Still of last night's vodka and bitters.
The windchimes' echo of whatever
Can't be seen. The bottlebrush
Has given up its hundred ghosts,
Each blossom a pinhead firmament,
Galaxies held in place by bristles
That sweep up the pollinated light

In their path along the season.
A scrub jay's Big Bang, the swarming
Dharma of gnats, nothing disturbs
The fixed orders but a reluctant question:
Is the world half-empty or half-full?
Through the leaves, traffic patterns
Bring the interstate to a light
Whose gears a semi seems to shift
With three knife-blade thrusts, angry
To overtake what moves on ahead.
This tree's broken under the day.
The red drips from stem to stem.
That wasn't the question. It was,
Why did we forget to talk about love?
We had all the time in the world.

What we forgot, I heard a voice
Behind me say, was everything else.
Love will leave us alone if we let it.
Besides, the world has no time for us,
The tree no questions of the flower,
One more day no help for all this night.

LATE NIGHT ODE

HORACE IV.i

It's over, love. Look at me pushing fifty now,
    Hair like grave-grass growing in both ears,
The piles and boggy prostate, the crooked penis,
    The sour taste of each day's first lie,

And that recurrent dream of years ago pulling
    A swaying bead-chain of moonlight,
Of slipping between the cool sheets of dark
    Along a body like my own, but blameless.

What good's my cut-glass conversation now,
    Now I'm so effortlessly vulgar and sad?
You get from life what you can shake from it?
    For me, it's g and t's all day and C N N.

Try the blond boychick lawyer, entry level
    At eighty grand, who pouts about the overtime,
Keeps Evian and a beeper in his locker at the gym,
    And hash in tinfoil under the office fern.

There's your hound from heaven, with buccaneer
    Curls and perfumed war-paint on his nipples.
His answering machine always has room for one more
    Slurred, embarrassed call from you-know-who.

Some nights I've laughed so hard the tears
    Won't stop. Look at me now. Why *now*?
I long ago gave up pretending to believe
    Anyone's memory will give as good as it gets.

So why these stubborn tears? And why do I dream
  Almost every night of holding you again,
Or at least of diving after you, my long-gone,
  Through the bruised unbalanced waves?

A NOTE ABOUT THE AUTHOR

J. D. McClatchy is the author of three earlier books of poems: *Scenes from Another Life* (1981), *Stars Principal* (1986) and *The Rest of the Way* (1990). His literary essays are collected in *White Paper* (1989) and *Twenty Questions* (1998). He has edited a number of books, including *The Vintage Book of Contemporary American Poetry* (1990) and *The Vintage Book of Contemporary World Poetry* (1996). He has written four opera libretti, most recently *Emmeline* for Tobias Picker, commissioned by the Santa Fe Opera. He is a Chancellor of the Academy of American Poets, and since 1991 he has been editor of *The Yale Review*.

A NOTE ON THE TYPE

This book was set in a typeface called Mrs. Eaves, a new design by Zuzana Licko. It is modeled after the work of John Baskerville but named for Sarah Eaves, who became his wife after the death of her first husband. This interpretation attempts to recreate the irregularity of metal typesetting and letterpress printing while abandoning Baskerville's sharp contrast between thick and thin strokes, which was much criticized in its time. To retain the open feeling of the letters, the width of the characters has been increased and the x-height reduced.

Zuzana Licko is a type designer with more than thirty typeface families to her credit. She is a cofounder of Emigre, a pioneer digital type foundry.

Composed by Creative Graphics, Allentown, Pennsylvania

Printed letterpress by The Stinehour Press, Lunenburg, Vermont

Bound by The Book Press, Brattleboro, Vermont

Designed by Chip Kidd and Misha Beletsky